Easter 91

A 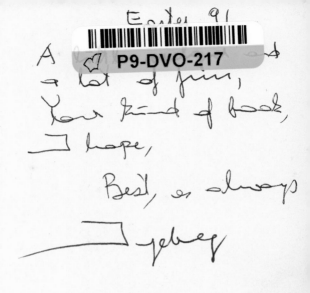 ... ...
... lot of fun,
Your kind of book,
I hope,

Best, as always

Digby

The Truth About Dogs

THE TRUTH ABOUT DOGS
Volker Kriegel

Translated and introduced by
Julian Barnes

WHISKY SMELLS LIKE DOG SMELLS LIKE WHISKY SMELLS LIKE DOG SMELLS LIKE WHISKY SMELLS

1817

HARPER & ROW, PUBLISHERS, New York
Cambridge, Philadelphia, San Francisco, London
Mexico City, São Paulo, Sydney

For Ev
but also for Juli, Nico, Joles
and all the others

Introduction

The trenchant and beguiling masterpiece you are about to
enjoy has three shameful British prejudices to overcome.
The first is our sturdy belief that the Germans, while
objects of ripe mirth in themselves, are incapable of being
funny. The second is our shockingly tolerant notion that a
collection of badly drawn cartoons can be just as amusing
as a book of well-drawn ones. And the third is our
incomprehensible addiction to books about cats.

The British have always asserted that the German sense
of humour is about as real as the Swiss Navy (though
personally I've always assumed that the prudent Swiss
kept a small flotilla tucked away somewhere in the
Mediterranean, just in case). This fairly harmless conten-
tion can be comforting, even necessary – look, they may
have all the Deutschmarks and most of the BMWs but
we're the ones with the sense of humour; yet it's getting
harder and harder to defend. For many years my own
prejudice was just as reliable as the next person's, despite
growing evidence that the Germans had in fact figured out
how to laugh. At first we admitted that, oh, sure, they
knew about being *satirical* (Grosz, Brecht/Weill and all
that). Irony? Yes, they might have mastered that. OK,
they could be scurrilous. Mocking? Yup. Gently droll?
Well, perhaps so (didn't *Heimat* surprise us?). Ah, but
could they be *funny*? This zig-zagging tactical retreat went
on for a long time and depended, of course, on the
constant redefinition of *funny* in terms of what the Germans were *not*.

I finally surrendered this increasingly hopeless position

last year in the departure lounge of Hamburg airport. It was six o'clock on a gloomy evening incorrectly billed as Spring. It had rained all day; I had seen nothing of Hamburg except through the spattered window of a car; I had read my work to a gathering of forty in an auditorium better suited to one of Hitler's medium-sized rallies; I had failed to sell a single copy of any of my books; and I had been paid just about enough to cover my duty-free. Now I was sitting with a clanking plastic bag among cheery Eurobusinessmen who knew much better than me how to vend their wares, and gazing out of the window at the low cloud, the steady rain, the skiddy runway. Idly, and without expectation, I picked up *Kriegels Kleine Hunde-Kunde* which someone had thrust on me after my reading. Within five pages I was restored to good humour; within ten I was snorting with laughter and a stranger to embarrassment; within twenty I was putting the book away for fear that Lufthansa would turn me back at the departure gate on the ground that I'd taken a dangerous dose of stimulants.

So I had. However, I had discovered not just a very funny cartoonist but also a draughtsman of rich variation and cunning line. Two of the more dismaying recent trends in Humour have been the rise of the cartoonist who can't draw and the tyranny of the caption. The first indicates a crazy democratization of the profession – everyone has a few cartoons inside them, along with the inevitable, unpublishable novel; the second is a nefarious vogue which can perhaps be traced back to the *New Yorker*. The cartoons in that magazine are extremely funny, but too often represent the triumph of the caption-writer (or a caption-rewriter like Peter de Vries). The draughtsman's contribution may be no more than de-lineating the frown of a husband and the glare of a wife, or vice versa: the drawings are merely there to set you up for the captions. In Volker Kriegel's work, the captions set you up for the drawings, and the drawings make you laugh. This seems to me the right way round.

So we are now in the presence of a genuinely funny German cartoonist who draws beautifully. The final problem is: he's chosen to depict dogs. This might not seem a difficulty, given that the British are famous dog-owners, dog-lovers, dog-shampooers, dog-buriers, and so on. But it is. In this country there are approximately six million dogs and six million cats; yet this equality of love and purchase is quite forgotten as soon as a member of our nation goes into a bookshop. When Mr Desmond Morris produced two companion volumes called *Dogwatching* and *Catwatching*, he found that the latter outsold the former in a ratio of two to one. *Catwatching* was even discovered selling well at dog shows. Why should ·this be? Are cat-owners more literate? Do they all live in city flats with potted plants and buy the latest paperbacks, whereas dog-owners live down muddy lanes miles from the nearest bookshop? Is there some connection between curling up with a cat and curling up with a book? Is dog-exercising a thorough psychological substitute for reading? Do cats like the quiet rustle of a turning page and dogs prefer the more vigorous stimulation of television? Do dogs bully their owners into not reading? Do dogs eat books? These are all matters requiring serious study.

This book tells you the truth about dogs, truth which is tender as well as sardonic. Dogs, for all their considerable faults, are what they are, and do not pretend otherwise; it is their owners who are devious, unpredictable, embarrassed and sentimental. The human race is distinctly fortunate that dogs have not yet learned how to blush. Volker Kriegel's little book is steeped in canine knowledge and drawn with the full growl of infuriated affection. It goes without saying that Herr Kriegel is himself a dog-owner; indeed, three-quarters of the dedicatees of this work have four legs and a tail. I suggest that *The Truth About Dogs* be put on sale at all cat shows.

Julian Barnes

12   Dogs are noisy

14   Dogs shit everywhere

16   Dogs have fleas

18 Dogs like to throw up on the carpet

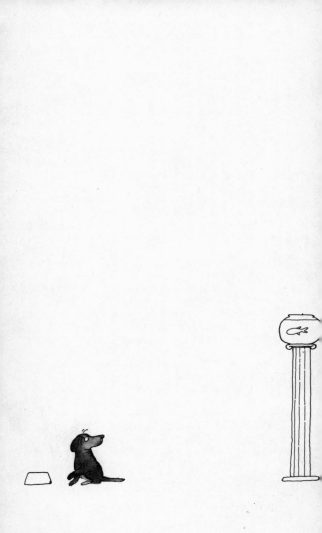

20   Dogs are gluttons

Dogs behave like the worst male chauvinist

Dogs have bad breath

Dogs fart

Dogs are dim

Dogs are demonstrative

32   Dogs stink

Dogs are sentimental   33

Dogs are playful

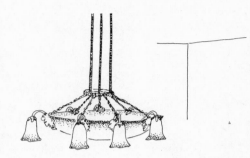

Dogs ask for trouble 39

A Comparison of Breeds I

A Comparison of Breeds II

The Natural Enemies of the Dog

a)

b)

c)

. . . not forgetting:

d) The Jogger

54 Dogs can be bribed

56 Dogs hide their smelly bones all over the place

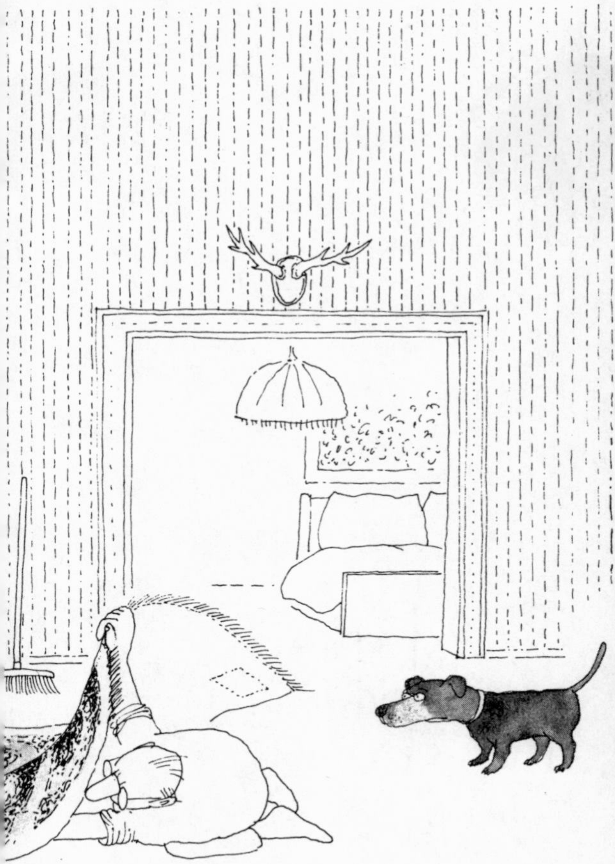

Dogs have little ear for music

60   Dogs ruin every holiday

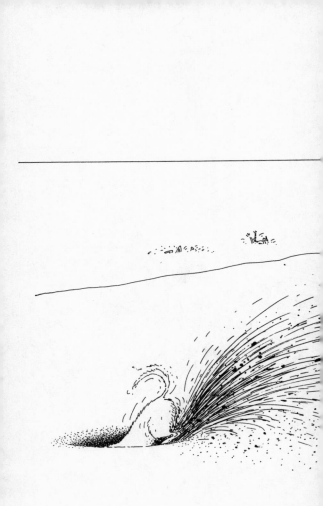

63

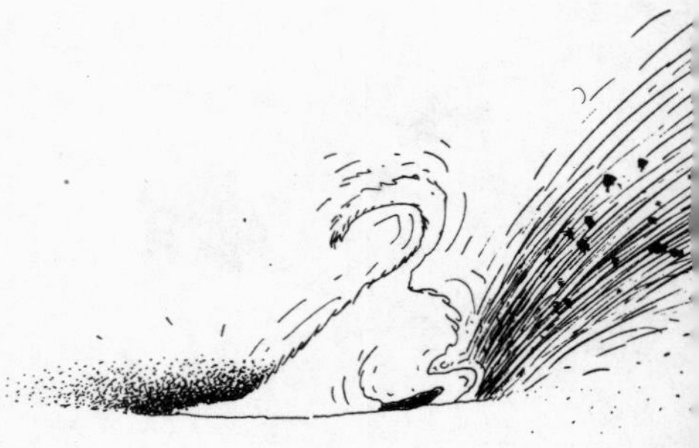

 . . . after year

66   Dogs really love to eat socks

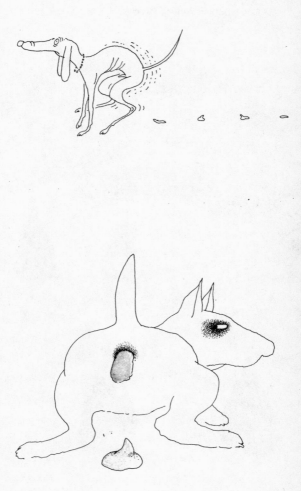

'The fascinating thing about him is his directness, his spontaneity, his – how can I put it? – his unruliness, that whiff of anarchy, that . . . forgive me, my dear . . . that proletarian aroma.'

'Sure, he's as stubborn as an old goat – does precisely as he pleases – loves rolling in shit – loses his hair like mad – you keep finding it on the sofa and the pillows – my trousers and coat are covered in it – and of course he's filthy, well, they all are – and he drools like an imbecile, and it's incredible the way he's always got slobber hanging out of his gob – plus which he gets me out of bed at half five every morning – *and* he's just taken up snoring – but, you know, in spite of it all, believe it or not, he's got . . . something – yes, when all's said and done, he's really got . . . something'

'Relax. It's just he can smell you're afraid of him.' 75

AND SOMETIMES
HE HAS THIS REALLY
FUNNY LOOK

LIKE WH

iKE THiS!

YES, i SEE WHAT YOU MEAN —
THAT'S **VERY** FUNNY

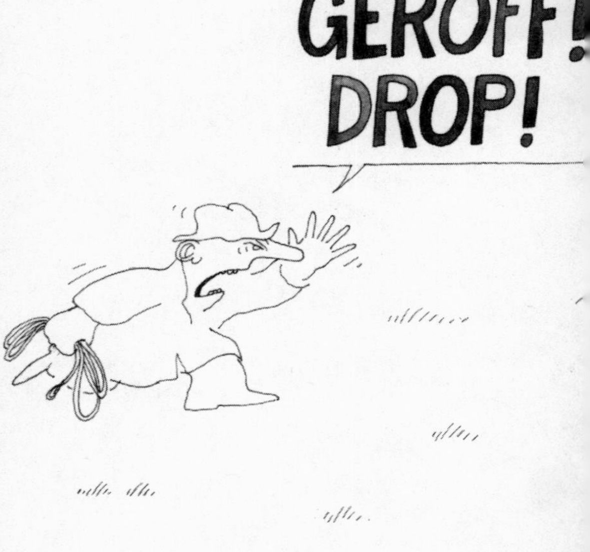
GEROFF!
DROP!

79

'It's the ideological side of things that really gets me. The fact is, the psychopathology of dogs is riddled with crypto-Fascist elements. It's revolting how easily they get fixated on some Führer figure. And then there's the whole business of precedence, hierarchy, authority, obedience – it's all extremely sinister. Of course they do need a firm hand. You don't get anywhere with anti-authoritarian sweet-talking. Only a couple of days ago, I was *forced* to punish him, right in the middle of the street, for getting into a fight with another dog. I'd only given him the slightest of taps on the rump with a copy of the *Guardian* when a couple of cretins started accusing me of being an author-itarian pig and cruelty to animals. Someone even called me a sadist. This damn dog is making me play a role I really hate. I can't take it any more.'

84   Dogs like to pee behind the sofa

There are dogs which are quite happy, long after their first youth has fled, to play the fool in exchange for a mere inch of spaghetti

86   Dogs are jealous

1)

PRINCE !

2)

HERE,
PRINCE!

3)

PRINCE !!
COME
HERE
THIS
INSTANT!

4)

GET A
MOVE ON

5)

6)

AND WHAT CAN
THE LITTLE
DOGGIE DO?

7)

CLEVER BOY,
PRINCE

Towards the close of the twentieth century
dogs increasingly took over those positions and functions
traditionally allotted to children

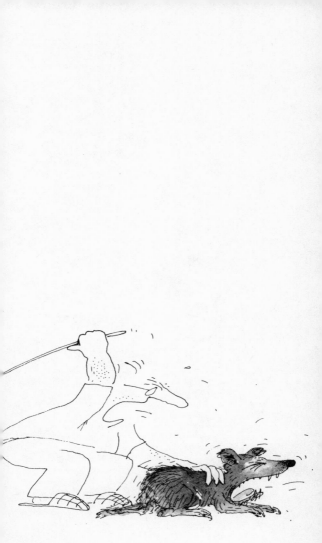

The Dog and the Car.

That's another story . . .

Dogs are flash

. . . not to mention
The Dog and the Motorbike

Famous Dog-Owners and their Pets

Adolf H. ('The Führer') with his alsatian ('Prince')

Frederick II ('The Great') with his greyhound ('Serge')   109

Arthur S. ('Schopi') with his poodle ('Atma' aka 'Butz')

Elizabeth II ('The Queen') with two of her 111
corgis ('Myth' and 'Fable')

Dogs have to be walked every single day

. . . and in absolutely every weather

Dogs can get very old